THE 5 CHORD SONGBOOK

Bob Dylan • Van Morrison • Zac Brown Band

Jason Mraz • The Lovin' Spoonful • Barry McGuire

Poison • Jack Johnson • Lenny Kravitz • John Denver

The McCoys • Jimi Hendrix • The Beatles • Bobby Darin

G	C		G	C		G	C	G	C

Sunshine on my shoulders makes me happy,

G	C		G	C			Am7	D7	

Sunshine in my eyes can make me cry.

The Goo Goo Dolls • Jimmie Rodgers

Journey • Rod Stewart • Lou Reed • John Mayer

Simon & Garfunkel • Guns N' Roses • The Byrds

The Irish Rovers • The Rooftop Singers

Cherry Lane Music Company
Director of Publications/Project Editor: Mark Phillips

ISBN 978-1-60378-395-8

Visit our website at www.cherrylaneprint.com

CONTENTS

Blowin' in the Wind

Words and Music by Bob Dylan

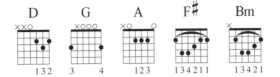

Verse 1

   D   **|G**   **|D**   **|**
How many roads must a man walk down

 |D   **|G**   **|A**   **|**
Be - fore you call him a man?

   |D   **|G**   **|D**   **|**
Yes, 'n' how many seas must a white dove sail

 |D   **|G**   **|A**   **|**
Be - fore she sleeps in the sand?

    |D   **|G**   **|D**   **|**
Yes, 'n' how many times must the cannon balls fly

 |D   **|G** **|A**
Be - fore they're forever banned?

   |G   **|A**   **|D**   **F#** **|Bm**
The answer, my friend, is blowin' in the wind,

  |G   **|A**   **|D**   **|**   **||**
The answer is blowin' in the wind.

Verse 2

D |G |D |

How many times must a man look up

  |D |G |A |

Be - fore he can see the sky?

    |D |G |D |

Yes, 'n' how many ears must one man have

  |D |G |A |

Be - fore he can hear people cry?

    |D |G |D |

Yes, 'n' how many deaths will it take till he knows

  |D |G |A |

That too many people have died?

   |G |A |D   F♯ |Bm

The answer, my friend, is blowin' in the wind,

  |G |A |D | ||

The answer is blowin' in the wind.

Verse 3

D |G |D |

How many years can a mountain ex - ist

  |D |G |A |

Be - fore it's washed to the sea?

    |D |G |D |

Yes, 'n' how many years can some people ex - ist

  |D |G |A |

Be - fore they're al - lowed to be free?

    |D |G |D |

Yes, 'n' how many times can a man turn his head,

  |D |G |A |

Pre - tending he just doesn't see?

   |G |A |D   F♯ |Bm

The answer, my friend, is blowin' in the wind,

  |G |A |D | ||

The answer is blowin' in the wind.

Brown Eyed Girl

Words and Music by
Van Morrison

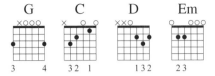

Intro   G |C |G |D |G |C |G |D   ‖

Verse 1

G |C |
Hey, where did we go?

G |D |
Days when the rains   came,

G |C |
Down in the hol - low,

G |D |
Playing a new   game.

G |C |
Laughing and a-running, hey, hey,

G |D |
Skipping and a-jumping.

G |C
In the misty morn - ing fog

|G |D |C |
With   our, hearts a-thumping, and you,

D |G |Em |
My brown-eyed girl.

C |D |G |D   ‖
You, my   brown-eyed girl.

Verse 2

```
G              |C          |
And  whatever  hap - pened
G                     |D         |
 To Tuesday and so    slow?
G                    |C              |
 Going down the old   mine with a
G            |D          |
 Transistor ra - dio.
G                  |C                |
 Standing in the sunlight laughing,
G              |D             |
 Hiding 'hind a rainbow's wall.
G                   |C          |
 Slipping and a-slid - ing
G            |D             |C           |
 All along the waterfall with you,
D            |G              |Em          |
 My brown-eyed girl.
C           |D         |G              |
 You, my     brown-eyed girl.
D7                |        |            ||
 Do you remem - ber when   we used to sing:
```

Chorus

```
G              |C             |G                |D            |
 Sha, la, la, la,  la, la, la, la,  la, la, la, te, da.   Just like that.
G            |C          |G                 |D
 Sha, la, la, la,  la, la, la, la,  la, la, la, te, da,
               |G        |          ||
La, te, da.
```

Interlude   G | | |C |G |D ||

Verse 3

G |C |
So hard to find my way

G |D |
Now that I'm all on my own.

G |C |
I saw you just the other day;

G |D |
My, how you have grown.

G |C |
Cast my memory back there, Lord.

G |D |
Sometimes I'm over - come thinking about it.

G |C |
Makin' love in the green grass

G |D |C |
Behind the stadium with you,

D |G |Em |
My brown-eyed girl.

C |D |G |
You, my brown-eyed girl.

D | | ||
Do you remem - ber when we used to sing:

Outro

G |C |G |D |
Sha, la, la, la, la, la, la, la, la, la, la, te, da.

G |C |G |D |G ||
Sha, la, la, la, la, la, la, la, la, la, la, te, da.

Chicken Fried

Words and Music by
Zac Brown and Wyatt Durrette

(Tune down one half step; low to high: E♭-A♭-D♭-G♭-B♭-E♭)

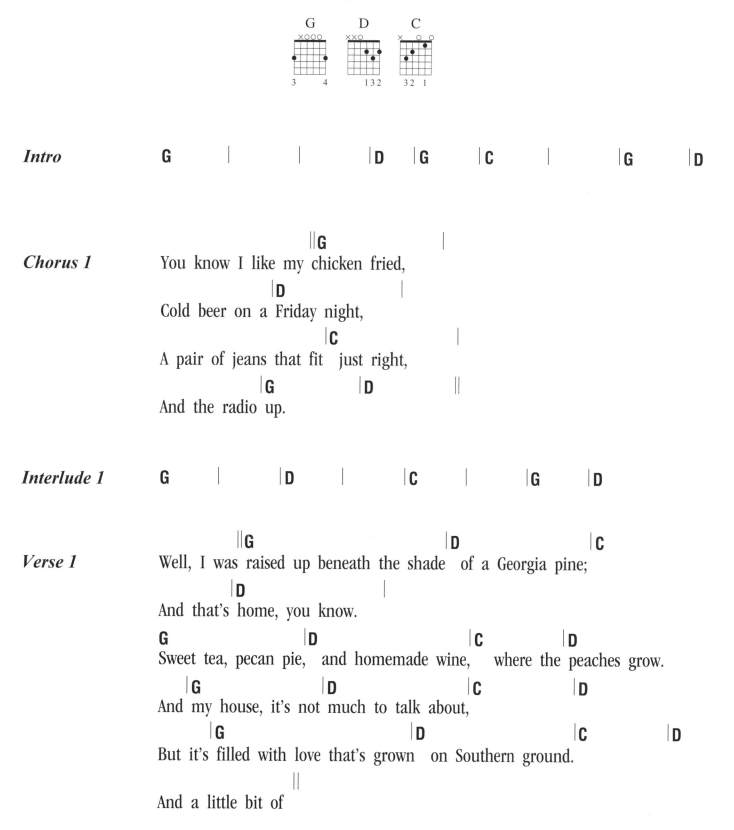

Intro   G | | |D |G |C | |G |D

Chorus 1
‖G |
You know I like my chicken fried,
|D |
Cold beer on a Friday night,
|C |
A pair of jeans that fit just right,
|G |D   ‖
And the radio up.

Interlude 1   G | |D | |C | |G |D

Verse 1
‖G |D |C
Well, I was raised up beneath the shade of a Georgia pine;
|D |
And that's home, you know.
G |D |C |D
Sweet tea, pecan pie, and homemade wine,   where the peaches grow.
|G |D |C |D
And my house, it's not much to talk about,
|G |D |C |D
But it's filled with love that's grown on Southern ground.
‖
And a little bit of

Chorus 2

G
Chicken fried,

|D
Cold beer on a Friday night,

|C
A pair of jeans that fit   just right,

|G   **|D**
And the radio up.

|G
I like to see the sunrise,

|D
See the love in my woman's eyes,

|C
Feel the touch of a precious child,

|G   **|D**
And know a mother's love.

Verse 2

||G   **|D**   **|C**   **|D**
It's funny how it's the little things in life   that mean the most;

|G   **|D**   **|C**   **|D**
Not where you live, what you drive, or the price tag on your clothes.

|G   **|D**   **|C**   **|D**
There's no dollar sign on peace of mind; this I've come to know.

|G   **|D**   **|C**   **|D**
So if you agree, have a drink with me, raise your glasses for a toast

||
To a little bit of

Repeat Chorus 2

Interlude 2

G		**	D**		**	C**	**	C**	**	G**	**	D**	
G		**	D**		**	C**	**	C**	**	G**	**	D**	
G			**	** D	G	**	C**		**	G**	**	D**

10

Verse 3

   ‖**G** |

I thank God for my life

     |**D** |

And for the Stars and Stripes.

        |**C** | |**G** |**D**

May freedom for - ever fly,   let it ring.

     |**G** |

Salute the ones who died,

       |**D** | |**C** |

The ones that give their lives   so we don't have to sacrifice

Tacet |**G** |**D**

All the things we love.   Like our

Repeat Chorus 2

Chorus 3

     ‖**G**

Get a little chicken fried,

      |**D** |

A cold beer on a Friday night,

       |**C** |

A pair of jeans that fit just right,

     |**G** |**D**

And the radio up.

     |**G** |

I like to see the sunrise,

     |**D** |

See the love in my woman's eyes,

     |**C** |

Feel the touch of a precious child,

     |**G** |**D** |**G** | **D** **G** ‖

And know a mother's love.

Curbside Prophet

Words and Music by
Jason Mraz, Billy Galewood and Christina Ruffalo

G   Csus2   Fmaj7   Gm/B♭   Dsus4/A

Intro

G   Csus2 |Fmaj7   Gm/B♭ Dsus4/A |

G   Csus2 |Fmaj7   Gm/B♭ Dsus4/A

Chorus 1

|| G   Csus2
I'm just a curbside prophet with my hand in my pocket,
|Fmaj7   Gm/B♭ Dsus4/A
And I'm waiting for my rocket to come.
|G   Csus2
I'm just a curbside prophet with my hand in my pocket,
|Fmaj7   Gm/B♭ Dsus4/A ||
And I'm waiting for my rocket, y'all.   Hey.

Interlude

G   Csus2 |Fmaj7   Gm/B♭ Dsus4/A |

G   Csus2 |Fmaj7   Gm/B♭ Dsus4/A

Verse 1

                   ‖**G**   **Csus2**
You see, it started way back in NY - C

          |**Fmaj7**   **Gm/B♭** **Dsus4/A**
When I stole my first rhyme from the M-I-C

        |**G**   **Csus2**
At-a West End Avenue at   Sixty-three.

           |**Fmaj7**   **Gm/B♭** **Dsus4/A** |**G**
It's the be - ginning of a leap year, Februar - y,   ninety - six,

                    Csus2
When a guitar, picked it up in the mix.

          |**Fmaj7**   **Gm/B♭**   **Dsus4/A**
I com - mitted to the licks a like a nickel bag of tricks.

          |**G**   **Csus2** |
Uh, well,   look at me now. Look at me now.

Fmaj7   **Gm/B♭**   **Dsus4/A**
Look at me now, now, now,   now.

Repeat Chorus 1

Repeat Interlude

Verse 2

        ‖**G**   **Csus2**
Well, then you'll never, da never, da guess what I bet,   bet, bet.

       |**Fmaj7**   **Gm/B♭**   **Dsus4/A** |
And I have   no regrets that I bet   my whole check - ing account,

G   **Csus2** |**Fmaj7**
  Because it all amounts   to nothing up in the end.

            Gm/B♭   **Dsus4/A** |**G**
Well, you can only count   that "On the Road Again"

             Csus2
Will soon be on my radio dial.

       |**Fmaj7**   **Gm/B♭**   **Dsus4/A**
And I been paying close attention to the Willie Nelson style.

     |**G**   **Csus2**
Like a,   a band of gypsies on the highway wild,

       |**Fmaj7**   **Gm/B♭**   **Dsus4/A** |
As I'm a one man mission on the California skyline.

G   **Csus2**
Drive up the coast and I brag and I boast

       |**Fmaj7**   **Gm/B♭**   **Dsus4/A** |
Because I'm picking up my pace. I'm makin' time like Space Ghost.

G   **Csus2** |
Raising a toast to the high - way patrol at the most,

Fmaj7   **Gm/B♭**   **Dsus4/A**
  But my cruise control's   on coast

      |**G**   **Csus2**
'Cause I'm tour'n' around the nation on ex - tended vacation.

      |**Fmaj7**   **Gm/B♭**   **Dsus4/A**
See I got Elsa, the dog who exceeds   my limi - tation.

     |**G**   **Csus2**
I say, "I like your style, crazy pound pup.

      |**Fmaj7**   **Gm/B♭**   **Dsus4/A**
You need a ride? Well, come on, girl. Hop in the truck."

Chorus 2

‖**G**   **Csus2**
With the curbside prophet with my hand in my pocket,

|**Fmaj7**   **Gm/B♭ Dsus4/A**
And I'm waiting for my rocket to come.

|**G**   **Csus2**
I'm just a curbside prophet with my hand in my pocket,

|**Fmaj7**   **Gm/B♭ Dsus4/A**
And I'm waiting for my rocket, y'all.

Repeat Chorus 2

Verse 3

‖**G**   **Csus2**
See, I'm a down home brother, red - neck undercover

|**Fmaj7 N.C.**
With my guitar here, I'm ready to play.

|**G**   **Csus2** |**Fmaj7 N.C.**
And I'm a sucker for a filly, got a natural ability geared   to freestyle.

|
Look at my flexibility.

G   **Csus2**
Dangerous on the mic, my ghetto hat's cocked right.

|**Fmaj7 N.C.**
All the ladies say, "Yo, that kid is crazy."

|**G**   **Csus2**
We got the backstage Betty's taking more than they can get.

|**Fmaj7 N.C.**   **Gm/B♭**
They say,   "What's up with M-R-A-Z."

Outro

      Dsus4/A ‖**G**   **Csus2**
Uh, hey, hey, hey, hey. Uh, hey.

     |Fmaj7   **Gm/B♭**   **Dsus4/A**
Some   -   thing's different in my world today.

       |G   **Csus2**   **|Fmaj7**   **Gm/B♭ Dsus4/A**
Well, they changed my traffic   signs to a brighter yellow.

     |G   **Csus2**
Uh, hey, hey.

     |Fmaj7   **Gm/B♭**   **Dsus4/A**
Some   -   thing's different in my world today.

       |G   **Csus2**   **|Fmaj7**   **Gm/B♭ Dsus4/A**
Well, they changed my traffic   signs to a brighter yellow.

       |G   **Csus2**
I'm just a curbside proph - et, love,

   |Fmaj7   **Gm/B♭**   **Dsus4/A**
A curbside brother,   love,

   |G   **Csus2**
A curbside brother,   love,

   |Fmaj7   **Gm/B♭**   **Dsus4/A |G**   ‖
A curbside … Oh,   come on.

Eve of Destruction

Words and Music by
P.F. Sloan and Steve Barri

D   G   A   Bm

Verse 1

```
  ‖D        |G      A        |
The Eastern world,   it is ex-ploding,
  D            |G              A
   Violence flaring,   and bullets load-ing.
        |D          |G        A
You're old enough to kill,  but not for voting.
        |D              |G              A
You don't believe in war, but what's that gun you're toting?
        |D              |G      A
And even the Jordan River has   bodies floating!
```

Chorus 1

```
       ‖D      |
But you  tell me
G       A      |D              |Bm
Over and o-ver and o-ver again, my friend,
        |G          |A
Ah, you don't believe we're on the eve
        |D      |      |G    |A      ‖
Of de-struction.
```

Verse 2

```
        D                           |G            A        |
Don't you understand what I'm  trying to say?
        D                         |G        A
Can't you feel the fears I'm  feeling to - day?
        |D                          |G            A
If the button is pushed, there's no  running away.
            |D                    |G              A
There'll be no one to save with the world in a grave.
        |D                     |G               A
Take a look around you, boy; it's bound to scare you, boy.
```

Chorus 2

```
            ||D          |
And you   tell me
    G       A      |D                    |Bm
Over and o - ver and o - ver again, my friend,
        |G              |A
Ah, you don't believe we're on the eve
        |D      |        |G      |A        |D        |      ,
Of de - struction.
```

Verse 3

```
            ||D                 |G          A      |
Yeah, my blood's so mad, feels like coagu - lating.
    D             |G      A
I'm sitting here just  contem - plating.
    |D                    |G              A
I can't twist the truth; it knows no regu - lation.
    |D                      |G          A
A handful of senators don't pass legis - lation,
        |D                |G          A
And marches alone can't bring inte - gration.
        |D             |G      A
When human respect is disinte - grating,
        |D             |G          A
This whole crazy world is just too frus - trating.
```

Repeat Chorus 2

Verse 4

‖D |G   A
And think of all the hate there is in Red Ch - ina.

   |D |G   A |
Then take a look around to Selma, Ala - bama.

D |G   A
You may leave here for four days in space,

   |D |G   A
But when you return, it's the same old place.

   |D |G   A
The pounding of the drums, the pride and disgrace,

    |D |G   A
You can bury your dead, but don't leave a trace.

     |D |G   A
Hate your next-door neighbor, but don't forget to say grace.

Chorus 3

   ‖D |
And tell me

G   A |D |Bm
Over and o - ver and o - ver and over again,   my friend,

  |G |A
You don't believe we're on the eve

    |D |
Of de - struction.

  |G |A
You don't believe we're on the eve

    |D | |G |D   ‖
Of de - struction.

Do You Believe in Magic

Words and Music by
John Sebastian

Dm7   Em7   F   G   C

Intro

| Dm7   Em7 | F   Em7 | Dm7   Em7 | |

Verse 1

    F   G || C |F
Do you be - lieve in mag - ic in a young girl's heart,

      |C |F
How the music can free her when - ever it starts?

      |C |F
And it's magic, if the music is groovy.

    |C |F
It makes you feel happy like an old-time movie.

    |Dm7   Em7 |F   Em7
I'll tell you 'bout the magic and it'll free your soul,

      |G | |
But it's like tryin' to tell a stranger 'bout   rock-and-roll.

Verse 2

                      || C |F
If you believe in mag - ic, don't you bother to choose

    |C |F
If it's jug band music or rhythm and blues.

              |C |F
Just go and listen; it'll start with a smile

         |C |F
That won't wipe off your face no matter how hard you try.

    |Dm7   Em7 |F   Em7
Your feet start tappin' and you can't seem to find

    |G | ||
How you got there, so just   blow your mind.

Interlude   F | |C | |

F   Em7 |F   Em7 |G |

                                          ||C |F
Verse 3   If you believe in mag - ic, come a - long with me.
                    |C |F
               We'll dance until morning till there's just you and me.
                    |C |F
               And maybe if the music is right,
                    |C |F
               I'll meet you tomorrow, sort of late at night.
                    |Dm7   Em7 |F   Em7
               And we'll go dancin', baby; then you'll see
                         |G | ||
               How the magic's in the music and the music's in me.

               F |
Outro   Yeah,

                              |C |
               Do you believe in mag - ic?
                    |F   Em7 |F   Em7
               Be - lieve in the magic of a young girl's soul?
                    |F   Em7 |F   Em7
               Be - lieve in the magic of rock-and-roll?
                    |F   Em7 |F   Em7 |G |
               Be - lieve in the magic that can set you free?
                    |F | |C |
               Do you believe like I believe? Do you believe like I believe?
                    |F | |C |
               Do you believe like I believe? Do you believe like I believe?
                    |F | |C | ||
               Do you believe like I believe?

Every Rose Has Its Thorn

Words and Music by
Bobby Dall, C.C. Deville, Bret Michaels and Rikki Rockett

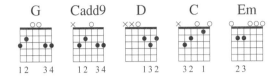

Intro   G |Cadd9 |G |Cadd9   ‖

Verse 1

G |Cadd9
    We both lie silently still in the dead of the night.

     |G |Cadd9
Although we both lie close together, we feel miles apart inside.

     |G   Cadd9
Was it some - thing I said or some   - thing I did?

     |G   Cadd9
Did my words   not come out right,

    |D |C
Though I tried   not to hurt you, though I tried?

     ‖
But I guess that's why they say:

Chorus

G |Cadd9

Every rose has its thorn,

           |G |Cadd9

Just like ev - 'ry night has its dawn.

           |G   D |Cadd9   G |

Just like ev - 'ry cow - boy sings his sad,   sad song,

G |Cadd9 ||

Every rose has its thorn.

Interlude   G |Cadd9   G |Cadd9

Verse 2

        ‖G |Cadd9

I listen to our favorite song playing on the radio,

            |G |Cadd9

Hear the dee - jay say love's a game of easy come and   easy go.

          |G   Cadd9

But I won - der, does he   know,

         |G   Cadd9

Has he ev - er felt like this?

        |D

And I know   that you'd be here right now

       |C ||

If I   could have let you know somehow. I guess

Repeat Chorus

Bridge

```
      Em                              D
         Though it's been awhile     now,

              |C                        G              |
      I can still   feel so much pain.

      Em                     D                           |
         Like a knife that cuts   you, the wound heals,

      C                                    |G      |Cadd9   |G      |Cadd9    ||
         But the scar, that scar remains.
```

Verse 3

```
      G                                            |Cadd9                        |
         I know I could have saved our love that night if I'd      known what to say.

      G                                  |Cadd9
         Instead of makin' love, we both      made our separate ways.

              |G                    Cadd9
      But now I    hear you found some - body new

       |G                  Cadd9
      And that I never meant that much to you.

          |D
      To hear that tears me up inside,

          |C                              ||
      And to see you cuts me like a knife. I guess
```

Repeat Chorus

24

Flake

Words and Music by Jack Johnson

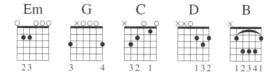

Verse 1

Em |G |
I know she said it's al - right,

C |G |
But you can make it up next time.

Em |G |
I know she knows it's not   right;

C |G |
There ain't no use in ly - ing.

Em |G
Maybe she thinks I know   something,

              |C |G |
Maybe, may - be she thinks it's fine.

Em |G
Maybe she knows something   I don't.

        |C |D ||
I'm so, I'm so tired,   I'm so tired of trying.

Chorus

```
        G                           |D              |
          It  seems  to  me  that  "may - be,"

        Em                              |B          |
          It  pretty  much  always  means   "no."

            |C          |D                |G    |D      |
        So  don't  tell  me  you  might;  just  let  it  go.

        G                       |D          |
          And  oftentimes  we're  la - zy;

        Em                          |B
          It  seems  to  stand  in  my   way.

            |C                    |D
        'Cause  no  one,  no,  not  no   one

                                |G      |D      ||
        Likes  to  be  let  down.
```

Verse 2

```
        Em                          |G          |
        I  know  she  loves  the  sun - rise,

        C                           |G              |
          No  longer  sees  it  with  her  sleeping  eyes  and…

        Em                              |G
          I  know  that  when  she  said  she's  gonna  try,

            |C                    |G                  |
        Well,  it  might   not  work  because  of  other  ties  and….

        Em                              |G          |
          I  know  she  usually  has  some  other  ties,  and

        C                               |G                          |
          I  wouldn't  want  to  break  'em,  nah,   I  wouldn't  want  to  break  'em.

        Em                      |G
          Maybe  she'll  help  me  to  untie  this,

            |C              |D                          ||
        But   until  then,  well,    I'm  gonna  have  to  lie,  too.
```

Repeat Chorus

26

```
G                              |D          |
…It seems to me that "may - be,"

Em                               |B
    It pretty much always means "no."

      |C            |D              |G        |D
So don't  tell me you might; just let it go.
```

Outro

```
        ‖G                                    |C
(The) harder that you try, baby, the further you'll fall,

        |G                  |D          |
Even with all  the money in the whole  wide world.

G                          |
Please, please, please don't pass me…

C                              |
Please, please, please don't pass me…

D          C                  |G
Please, please, please don't pass me by.

      |G                                          |C
Everything you know about me now, baby, you gonna have to change,

              |G                  |D          |
You gonna have to call  it by a brand-new name,  oo, oo, oo.

G                              |
Please, please, please don't drag me…

C                                  |
Please, please, please don't drag me…

D          C                      |G
Please, please, please don't drag me down.

        |G                                      |C
Just like a tree  down by the water, baby, I shall not move,

          |G              |D          |
Even after all the silly things you do, oo, oo, oo,

G                              |
Please, please, please don't drag me…

C                                  |
Please, please, please don't drag me…

D          C                      |G      |          ‖
Please, please, please don't drag me down.
```

F-Stop Blues

Words and Music by Jack Johnson

E   B   A   G#m   F#m

Verse 1

E   B
Hermit crabs and cow - ry shells

           |A
Crush be - neath his feet as he comes towards you.

    |E   B |A
He's   wav - ing at you.

    |E   B |
Lift him up to see what you can see.

A
He begins his focusing.

    |E   B |
He's   aim - ing at you.

A |E   B
    And now he has cutaways from mem - ories

    |A |
And   close-ups of anything that

E   B |
He has seen or e - ven dreamed.

A
And now he's finished focusing.

    |E   B |
He's imagining lightning

A |
Striking sea sickness

E   B |A ||
Away from here.

Chorus

E   G♯m
Look who's laughing now,

                  |A   B |
That you've   wast - ed,

E   G♯m |A   B |
How many years?   And you've barely even tast - ed

E   G♯m |
Anything remote - ly close to

A   B |
Everything you've boast - ed about.

E   G♯m |A   B   ‖
Look who's crying now.

Verse 2

E   B |
  Driftwood floats after years of erosion.

A |
Incoming tide touches roots to expose them.

E   B |
  Quicksand steals my shoes.

A |
  Clouds bring the f-stop blues.

F♯m |A   ‖

Repeat Chorus

Fly Away

Words and Music by
Lenny Kravitz

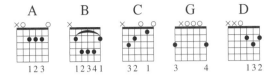

Intro

|A   B C |G   D |A   B C |G   D ||

Verse 1

A   B   C |G   D |
I wish that I could fly in-to the sky so very high,

A   B   C |G D |
Just like a dragonfly.

A   B   C |G   D |
I'd fly a-bove the trees, o-ver the seas, in all degrees,

A   B   C |G D ||
To an-ywhere I please.   Oh.

Chorus

A   B C |
I want to get away.

G   D |A B   C |G   D |
I want to fly away,   yeah, yeah, yeah.

A   B C |
I want to get away.

G   D |A B   C |G   D ||
I want to fly away,   yeah, yeah, yeah.

Verse 2

```
         A      B      C        |G         D          |
         Let's go and see the stars, the Milky Way or even Mars,

         A      B      C        |G D |
         Where it could just be ours.

         A      B      C        |G         D          |
         Let's fade in-to the sun, let your spirit fly where we are one,

         A      B   C   |G      D        ||
         Just for a lit-tle fun,  oh, oh,  oh, yeah.
```


Repeat Chorus (2X)

Outro

```
         A      B C        |G              D |
         I want to get away, I want to get away.

         A      B C        |G              D    |
         I want to get away, I want to get away,  yeah.

         A      B C        |G         D    |A B   C     |G
         I want to get away,  I want to fly  away,  yeah, yeah, yeah.

         D                      |
         Girl, I got to get away.

         A      B C        |G              D |
         I want to get away, I want to get away.

         A      B C        |G              D    |
         I want to get away, I want to get away,  yeah.

         A      B C        |G         D    |A B   C     |G
         I want to get away,  I want to fly  away,  yeah, yeah, yeah.

         D              |      ||
         Yeah, yeah, yeah, yeah, yeah.
```

For You

Words and Music by
John Denver

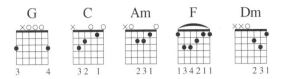

Verse 1

    G   **|C**   **|Am**
Just to look in your eyes again,

           |F   **|Dm**
Just to lay in your arms,

            |G   **|C**   **|G**
Just to be the first one always there for you.

          |C   **|Am**
Just to live in your laughter,

          |F   **|Dm**
Just to sing in your heart,

           |G   **|C**   **|**
Just to be every one of your dreams come true.

Verse 2

    G   **‖C**   **|Am**
Just to sit by your window,

          |F **|Dm**
Just to touch in the night,

         |G   **|C** **|G**
Just to offer a prayer each day for you.

          |C   **|Am**
Just to long for your kisses,

           |F   **|Dm**
Just to dream of your sighs,

          |G   **|C**   **|**
Just to know that I'd give my life for you.

Chorus 1

    G   ‖C |Am   F G
For you, all the rest   of my life.

    |C |Am   F G
For you, all the best   of my life.

    |C |G |C |
For you alone,   only for you.

Verse 3

          G   ‖C |Am
Just to wake up each morning,

         |F |Dm
Just to you by my side,

                |G |C |G
Just to know that you're never really far a-way.

         |C |Am
Just a reason for living,

         |F |Dm
Just to say I a-dore,

             |G |C |
Just to know that you're here in my heart to stay.

Chorus 2

    G   ‖C |Am   F G
For you, all the rest   of my life.

    |C |Am   F G
For you, all the best   of my life.

    |C |G |C   G ‖
For you alone,   only for you.

Outro   C |Am |F |Dm |G |C |G

             |C |Am
Just the words of a love song,

         |F |Dm
Just the beat of my heart,

              |G |C | ‖
Just the pledge of my life, my love, for you.

Hang On Sloopy

Words and Music by
Wes Farrell and Bert Russell

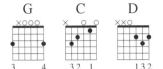

Chorus

G   C |D   C |G C |D C |
Hang   on Sloopy, Sloopy hang on.

G   C |D   C |G C |D C ||
Hang   on Sloopy, Sloopy hang on.

Verse 1

G   C |D   C |G C   D C
Sloopy lives in a very bad part of town.

 |G   C   D   C |G   C D C ||
And everybod‑y, yeah, tries to put my Sloopy down.

Verse 2

G   C |D   C |G C |D C
Sloopy, I don't care what your daddy do,

 |G   C |D   C |G C |D
'Cause you know, Sloopy girl, I'm in love with you.

            ||
And so I sing out:

Repeat Chorus

Verse 3

G   C |D   C |G   C |D   C |
Sloopy, let your hair down,   let it hang down on me.

G   C |D   C |G   C |D
Sloopy, let your hair down, girl,   let it hang down on me.

Interlude

C   ‖G   C |D
Come on, Sloopy. (Come on, come on.)

C |G   C |D
Come on, Sloopy. (Come on, come on.)

      C |G   C |D
Well, come on, Sloo-py. (Come on, come on.)

      C |G   C |D
Well, come on, Sloo-py. (Come on, come on.)

     C |G   C |D
Well, it feels so good. (Come on, come on.)

      C |G   C |D
You know it feels so good. (Come on, come on.)

       C |G   C |D
Well, shake it, shake it, shake it, Sloopy. (Come on, come on.)

     C |G   C |D | ‖
Well, shake it, shake it, shake it, yeah. (Come on, come on.)   Ahh!

Repeat Chorus

Hey Joe

Words and Music by
Billy Roberts

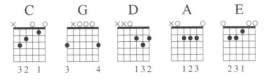

Verse 1

    C   **G** |
Hey, Joe,

D   **A** |**E** | |
Where you goin' with that gun in your hand?

    C   **G** |
Hey, Joe,

D   **A** |**E** | |
I said where ya goin' with that gun in your hand?

C   **G** |
I'm goin' down to shoot my old lady.

D   **A** |**E** | |
You know I caught her messin' 'round with an - other man.

C   **G** |
I'm goin' down to shoot my old lady,

D   **A** |**E**
You know I caught her messin' 'round with an - other man.

             |**E** ||
And that ain't too cool.

Verse 2

```
       C       G      |D         A
        Hey,  Joe,
                            |E                                            |              |
I heard you shot your woman down, you shot her down now.
       C      G      |D       A
        Hey,  Joe,
                          |E
I heard you shot your old lady down.
                                |E              |
You shot her down to the ground.          Yeah.
       C          G              |
        Yes, I  did, I  shot her.
       D       A                    |
        You know I caught her messin' 'round,
       E                    |                        |
Messin' 'round town.
       C          G              |
        Yes, I  did, I  shot her.
       D            A                          |E
        You know I caught my old lady messin' 'round town.
                        |E                    ||
And I gave her the gun.  I shot her!
```

Interlude

```
        C        G       |D       A       |E                    |                    |
        C        G       |D       A       |E                    |                    |
        C        G       |D       A       |E                    |                    ||
```

Verse 3

```
           C     G     |D         A
           Hey,  Joe,
                                |E                              |                    |
Where you gonna run to now, where you gonna run to?
           C     G        |D        A
           Hey,  Joe, I said
                              |E
Where you gonna run  to now,
                                   |E                        |
Where you, where you gonna go?       Well, dig it!
           C          G            |D        A
           I'm goin' way down south,
                          |E              |              |
Way down to Mexico way.        Alright.
           C          G            |D        A
           I'm goin' way down south,
                              |E
Way down where I  can be free.
                            |E              |
Ain't no one  gonna find me.
           C        G            |
           Ain't no hangman gonna,
           D           A              |E
           He ain't gonna put a rope around me.
                               |E                        |
You better believe it right  now.   I gotta go now.
           C     G     |D     A     |E            |              ||
```

38

Maggie May

Words and Music by
Rod Stewart and Martin Quittenton

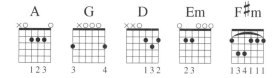

Verse 1

```
A                        |G                   |D                |
Wake up, Maggie, I think I got something to say to you.

     |A                  |G                |D                    |
It's late September and I really should be back at school.

|G                     |D
I know I keep you amused,

     |G              |A
But I feel I'm being used.

     |Em                    |F♯m    |Em       |        D
Oh Maggie, I couldn't have tried any more.

     |Em                  |A
You lured me away from home

       |Em                |A
Just to save you from being a - lone.

     |Em              |A              |D           |
You stole my heart and that's what really hurts.
```

Verse 2

|| A | G | D |

The morning sun when it's in your face really shows your age.

 | A | G | D |

But that don't worry me none; in my eyes you're everything.

 | G | D

I laughed at all of your jokes;

 | G | A

My love you didn't need to coax.

 | Em | F♯m | Em | D

Oh Maggie, I couldn't have tried any more.

 | Em | A

You lured me away from home

   | Em | A

Just to save you from being a - lone.

 | Em | A   G | D | ||

You stole my soul and that's a pain I can do without.

Verse 3

A | G | D |

All I needed was a friend to lend a guiding hand.

 | A | G | D |

But you turned into a lover and mother, what a lover; you wore me out.

 | G | D

All   you did was wreck my bed

   | G | A

And in the morning kick me in the head.

 | Em | F♯m | Em | D

Oh Maggie, I couldn't have tried any more.

 | Em | A

You lured me away from home

   | Em | A

'Cause you didn't want to be a - lone.

 | Em | A | D | ||

You stole my heart; I couldn't leave you if I tried.

Verse 4

```
A                      |G                          |D                           |
I suppose I could col - lect my books and get on back to school,

    |A              |G                          |D                    |
Or steal my daddy's cue and make a living out of playing pool.

    |G                          |D
Or find myself a rock-and-roll band

     |G                      |A
That needs a helpin' hand.

    |Em                      |F♯m            |Em          |    D
Oh Maggie, I wish I'd never seen your face.

              |Em                      |A
You made a first-class fool out of me,

            |Em                      |A
But I'm as blind as a fool can be.

    |Em                      |A        G        |D          |            ||
You stole my heart but I love you an - yway.
```

Outro

```
D       |Em    |G              |D        |      |Em      |G        |D
Maggie, I wish I'd never seen your face.

    |D            |Em    |G          |D        |      |Em      |G        |D      ||
I'll get on back home one of these days.
```

House of the Rising Sun

Southern American Folksong

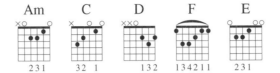

Verse 1

|Am |C |D |F
There is a house in New Orleans

      |Am |C |E |
They call the Rising Sun.

      |Am |C |D |F
It's been the ruin of many a poor girl,

      |Am |E |Am |E
And I, oh Lord, was one.

Verse 2

‖Am |C |D |F
My mother, she is a tailor,

      |Am |C |E |
She sells those new blue jeans.

      |Am |C |D |F
My sweetheart, he's a drunkard, Lord,

      |Am |E |Am |E
Drinks down in New Or - leans.

Verse 3

```
|| Am |C        |D       |F
The only thing a drunkard needs

   |Am      |C     |E     |
Is a suitcase and a trunk.

   |Am |C  |D       |F
The only time he's satis - fied

   |Am         |E    |Am    |E ||
Is when he's on a drunk.
```

Verse 4

```
Am            |C     |D       |F
One foot is on the platform,

      |Am        |C     |E     |
And the other one on the train.

   |Am |C      |D       |F
I'm going back to New Or - leans

   |Am       |E       |Am  |E
To wear that ball and chain.
```

Repeat Verse 1

I Saw Her Standing There

Words and Music by
John Lennon and Paul McCartney

E7   A7   B7   E   C

2 3 1 4   2 3   2 1 3 4   2 3 1   3 2 1

Verse 1

‖E7 |
Well, she was just   seventeen,

|A7 |E7
You know what I mean,

|E7 | |B7 |
And the way she looked was way beyond com - pare.

|E |E7 |A7 |C
So how could I dance with anoth - er,   woo,

|E7 |B7 |E7 |
When I saw her standing there?

Verse 2

‖E7 |
Well, she   looked at me,

|A7 |E7
And I,   I could see

|E7 | |B7 | |
That be - fore too long I'd fall in love with her.

E |E7 |A7 |C
She wouldn't dance with anoth - er,   woo,

|E7 |B7 |E7 |
When I saw her standing there.

Bridge

          ‖**A7** |
Well, my heart went boom

         |**A7** |
When I crossed that room

        |**A7** | **B7** | **A7** |
And I held her hand   in   mine.

Verse 3

            ‖**E7** |
Oh, we danced   through the night,

         |**A7** |**E7**
And we held each other tight,

         |**E7** | **B7** |
And be - fore too long I fell in love with her.

       |**E** |**E7** |**A7** |**C**
Now I'll never dance   with anoth - er,   woo,

        |**E7** |**B7** |**E7** | ‖
Since I saw her standing there.

Interlude

E7 | | | | | **B7** | |

E7 | **A7** | **E7**   **B7**   **E7** |

Repeat Bridge

Repeat Verse 3

         |**E7** |**B7** |**E7** |
Oh, since I saw her   standing there.

         |**E7** |**B7** |**A7** |**E7** | ‖
Yeah, well, since I saw her   standing there.

If I Were a Carpenter

Words and Music by
Tim Hardin

D   C   G/B

Verse 1

D ‖**C** |
If I were a carpenter

G/B |**D** |
And you were a lady,

D |**C** |
Would you marry me anyway,

G/B |**D** | |
Would you have my baby?

D |**C** |
If a tinker were my trade,

G/B |**D** |
Would you still find me,

D |**C** |
Carrying the pots I'd made,

G/B |**D** | |**C** **G/B** |**D** ‖
Following be - hind me?

Bridge

C |**D** |
Save my love through loneliness,

C |**D** |
Save my love for sorrow

D |**C** |
I've given you my ownliness;

G/B |**D** | | |
Come and give me your to - morrow.

Verse 2

```
D              ‖C           |
   If I worked my hands in wood
G/B          |D        |
   Would you still love me?
D                  |C          |
   Answer me, babe, "Yes, I would,
G/B          |D        |         |
   I'd put you a‑bove me."
D           |C        |
   If I were a miller
G/B              |D        |
   At a mill wheel grinding,
D                    |C          |
   Would you miss your colored blouse,
G/B              |D        |        |C   G/B  |D          ‖
   Your soft shoes shining?
```

Interlude

```
C       |G/B      |D      |        |C        |G/B      |D      |
```

Verse 3

```
D          ‖C         |
   If I were a carpenter
G/B                |D       |
   And you were a lady,
D                  |C        |
   Would you marry me anyway,
G/B                  |D       |        |        |        |
   Would you have my baby?
D                  |C        |
   Would you marry me anyway,
G/B                    |D       |      |C        |G/B  |D       |        ‖
   Would you have my baby?
```

Iris
from the Motion Picture CITY OF ANGELS

Words and Music by
John Rzeznik

D5   Em7   G5   Bm   Asus4

Verse 1

|D5 |Em7 |G5 |
And I'd give up for - ever to touch you,

|Bm |Asus4 |G5 |
'Cause I know that you feel me some - how.

|D5 |Em7 |G5 |
You're the closest to heaven that I'll ever be,

|Bm |Asus4 |G5 |
And I don't want to go home right now.

Verse 2

‖D5 |Em7 |G5 |
And all I can taste is this moment,

|Bm |Asus4 |G5 |
And all I can breathe is your life.

|D5 |Em7 |G5 |
'Cause sooner or later it's over.

|Bm |Asus4 |G5 |
I just don't want to miss you to - night.

Chorus

```
       ‖Bm              |Asus4     |G5           |
And  I  don't  want  the  world  to  see  me,

          |Bm                |Asus4          |G5              |
'Cause  I  don't  think  that  they'd  under - stand.

          |Bm          |Asus4      |G5           |
When  everything's  made  to  be  broken,

          |Bm              |Asus4        |G5            |
I  just  want  you  to  know  who  I  am.
```


Verse 3

```
          ‖D5             |Em7        |G5                 |
And  you  can't  fight  the  tears  that  ain't  coming

          |Bm          |Asus4       |G5               |
Or  the  moment  of  truth  in  your  lies.

          |D5          |Em7          |G5                 |
When  everything  feels  like  the  movies,

              |Bm              |Asus4            |G5               |
Yeah,  you  bleed  just  to  know  you're  a - live.
```


Repeat Chorus (2x)

Outro

```
          ‖Bm            |Asus4      |G5                |
I  just  want  you  to  know  who  I  am.

          |Bm          |Asus4       |G5            |
I  just  want  you  to  know  who  I  am.

          |Bm          |Asus4      |Bm            ‖
I  just  want  you  to  know  who  I  am.
```

Just a Closer Walk with Thee

Traditional
Arranged by Kenneth Morris

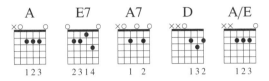

Verse 1

A |**E7** |
I am weak, but Thou art strong;
E7 |**A** |
Jesus, keep me from all wrong.
A   **A7** |**D**
I'll be satisfied as long
    |**A/E**   **E7** |**A** ||
As I walk, dear Lord, close to Thee.

Refrain

A |**E7** |
Just a closer walk with Thee;
E7 |**A** |
Grant it, Jesus, is my plea,
A   **A7** |**D**
Daily walking close to Thee,
    |**A/E**   **E7** |**A** ||
Let it be, dear Lord, let it be.

Verse 2

```
A                              |E7                   |
Through this world of toil and snares,
E7                        |A              |
If I falter, Lord, who cares?
A         A7              |D
Who with me my burden shares?
           |A/E      E7          |A              ||
None but Thee, dear Lord, none but Thee.
```

Repeat Refrain

Verse 3

```
A                              |E7                   |
When my feeble life is o'er,
E7                          |A              |
Time for me will be no more.
A         A7              |D
Guide me gently, safely o'er
           |A/E      E7          |A              ||
To Thy shore, dear Lord, to Thy shore.
```

Repeat Refrain

Kisses Sweeter Than Wine

Words by Ronnie Gilbert, Lee Hays, Fred Hellerman and Pete Seeger
Music by Huddie Ledbetter

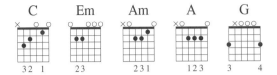

Chorus

C |Em|Am |A | |
Oh,   kisses sweeter than wine,

C |Em|Am |A |
Oh,   kisses sweeter than wine.

Verse 1

‖C   G |Am   Em
When I was a young man and never been kissed,

|G   Em |A
I got to thinkin' over what I had missed.

|C   G |Am   Em |
I got me a girl, kissed her and then,

G   Em |A   ‖
Oh, Lord, I kissed her again.

Repeat Chorus

Verse 2

‖C   G |Am   Em
He asked me to marry and be his sweet wife,

|G   Em |A
And we would be so happy all of our life.

|C   G |Am   Em |
He begged and he pleaded like a natural man and then,

G   Em |A   ‖
Oh Lord, I gave him my hand.

Repeat Chorus

Verse 3
```
       ‖C          G      |Am        Em
I worked mighty hard and so did my wife,

          |G     Em      |A
A - workin' hand in hand to make a good life.

     |C       G      |Am          Em            |
With corn in the fields and wheat in the bins and then,

G    Em          |A              ‖
Oh Lord, I was the father of twins.
```

Repeat Chorus

Verse 4
```
       ‖C     G      |Am        Em
Our children numbered just about four

       |G     Em          |A
And they all had sweethearts knock on the door.

     |C     G          |Am          Em          |
They all got married and they didn't wait, I was,

G    Em          |A                     ‖
Oh Lord, the grandfather of eight.
```

Repeat Chorus

Verse 5
```
       ‖C     G      |Am        Em
Now we are old and ready to go,

           |G           Em          |A
We get to thinking what happened a long time ago.

     |C       G      |Am          Em      |
We had lots of kids and trouble and pain, but

G    Em          |A              ‖
Oh Lord, we'd do it again.
```

Repeat Chorus

Lights

Words and Music by
Steve Perry and Neal Schon

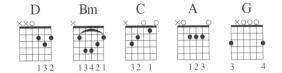

Chorus

|D   Bm |C
When the lights go down in the city

|D   Bm |C
And the sun shines on the bay,

|D   Bm |C |
Ooh, I want to be there   in my city, oh, oh,

Bm **C**   **|D** ||
Oh,   oh,   oh.

Verse

```
     D          Bm       |C              |
     So, you think you're  lonely.

     D             Bm      |C             |
     Well, my friend, I'm lonely too.

     D                Bm           |C                    |
     I want to get back to my city by the bay,

Bm             C         |D
Oh,                      oh.
```

Bridge

```
        ‖Bm  A  G              |D
It's sad,    oh, there's been mornings

                        |Bm          A   G
Out on the road with - out you,

                   |D       A        |
Without your charms,

Bm    A  G          |D                    |
   Oh,    oh, my, my, my, my, my, my.

Bm    C  |D
Woh,     oh.
```

Repeat Chorus

Plane

Words and Music by
Jason Mraz and Dennis Morris

(Tune down one half step; low to high: E♭-A♭-D♭-G♭-B♭-E♭)

Em	G	C	B7	D

Intro　　**Em　G　|C　B7　|Em　G　|C　B7　‖**

Verse 1

　　　　　　Em　　　　　　　　　G
Drain the veins in my head.
　　　　　　　　　|C　　　　　　　　B7　　　　|
Clean out the reds in my eyes to get　by security lines.
Em　　　　　　　G
　　Dear X-ray ma - chine,
　　　　　　　|C　　　　　　　B7　　　　　　　|
Pretend you don't know me so well. I won't tell if you lie.
Em　　　　　　　　　　　　G
Cry 'cause the drought's been brought up.
　　　　　　　　　|C　　　　　　　　B7
Drinkin' 'cause you're looking so good in your Star - bucks cup.
　　|Em　　　　　　　　　G
I com - plain for the company that I　keep.
　　　　　　|C　　　　　　　　　　B7
The window's for sleeping; rearrange. Well, I'm no - body.

Chorus 1

                      ||C

Well, who's laughing now?

              G |

I'm leaving your town again.

B7 |C

    And I'm over the ground that you've been spin - ning.

                             G |B7

And I'm up in the air,   so, baby, hell, yeah!

                                      |

Well, honey, I can see your house from here.

C   G |

    If the plane goes down,   damn,

B7 |

    Well, I'll remember where the love was found.

C   G |B7 ||

    If the plane goes down,   damn.

Verse 2

Em   G

Damn! I should be so lucky.

                    |C

Even only twen - ty-four hours under your touch,

B7

You know I need you so much.

  |Em   G |C

I,   I cannot wait to call you and tell you that I land - ed

                                    B7 |

Somewhere and hand you a square   of the airport

Em   G |

    And walk you through the maze of the map that I'm gazing at,

C   B7

Gracefully unnamed and feeling guilty

                                      |

For the luck and the look that you gave me.

Em   G

    You make me somebod - y.

                  |C   B7 ||

Oh, nobody knows   me. Not even me can see it, yet I bet I'm

Chorus 2

```
         C              G              |
         Leaving  your  town  again.
         B7                                    |C
         And  I'm  over  the  ground  that  you've  been  spin - ning.
                          G            |B7
         And  I'm  up  in  the  air,    so,  baby,  hell,  yeah!
                                             |
         Well,  honey,  I  can  see  your  house  from  here.
         C              G              |
         If  the  plane  goes   down,   damn,
         B7                                   |
         I'll  remember  where  the  love  was  found.
         C              G              |B7          ||
         If  the  plane  goes   down,   damn.
```

Interlude

```
         Em   D   |C          |Em   G   |C   B7
```

Bridge

```
                         ||Em   D         |C
         You  get  me  high  -  minded.
                            |Em   G   |C   B7      ||
         You  keep  me  high.
```

Verse 3

```
        Em              G                      |C
         Flax seeds,  well, they tear me o - pen
                                  B7                        |
And supposedly you could crawl right through me.
        Em            G                  |
         Taste  these  teeth,  please,
        C                        B7
         And undress me from the sweaters.
                                  |Em           G                |
Better hurry, 'cause I'm    heating upward bound now.
        C                    B7
         Oh, maybe I'll build my house on your cloud.
           |Em        G              |
Here I'm    tumbling     for you,
        C                                        B7                        ||
Stumbling through the work that I have to do. Don't mean to harm you
```

Chorus 3

```
        C                    G              |
         By leaving your town again.
B7                                                  |C
         But I'm over the quilt that you've been spin - ning.
                        G            |B7
And I'm up in the air,    so, baby, hell, yeah!
                                      |C
Well, honey, I can see your house from here.
                        G              |
If the plane goes down,    damn,
B7                                                  |
         I'll remember where the love was found.
        C                G                  |
         If the plane goes  down,    damn,
B7                                                  |
         I'll remember where the love was found.
        C          G                  |
         If the plane  goes down,    damn,
B7                                                  |
         I'll remember where the love was found.
        C          G                |B7                        ||
         If the plane  goes down,  damn,    damn,    damn.
```

Outro   Em   G |C   B7

        |Em   G |C   B7
Damn.

        |Em   G |C   B7
You get me high.

        |Em   G |C   B7
You keep me high - minded.

        |Em   G |C   B7
You get me high.

        |Em   G |C   B7 |Em ||
You get me high - minded.

Rock and Roll

Words and Music by
Lou Reed

Tune down one whole step:
(low to high) D-G-C-F-A-D

D   C   G   Em   A

Intro   D | C| | G| | D| | ||

Verse 1

D   C |
    Jenny said when she was just five years old,

G | D | | |
"You know, there's   nothin' happening at all."

D   C |
    Every time she put on   the radio

G | D | | |
There was noth - in' goin' down at all,   not at all.

D   C |
    One fine mornin' she puts on a New York station

G | D | | |
And she couldn't be - lieve what she heard at all.

D   C |
    She started dancin' to that fine, fine, fine, fine music.

G | D |
Oo,   her life was saved by rock 'n' roll.

    |D
Hey baby, rock 'n' roll.

Chorus

  ‖Em |G

De - spite all the amputa - tions,

    |A |G

You could dance to a rock 'n' roll station.

      |D   G |

And it was all right.

      |D   G | ‖

It was all right.   Hey, babe.

Interlude   D | C| | G| | D| | ‖

   D   C |

2nd Verse   Jenny said when she was just five years old,

       G | D | | |

"You know there's   nothin' happening at all."

D   C | G |

  Two TV sets, two Cadillac cars, aw,

       D | | |

It ain't helpin' us at all, not at all.

D   C | G |

  One fine morning she heard a New York sta - tion;

        D | | | ‖

She couldn't believe what she heard at all, not at all.

Chorus

Em |G

Despite the ampu - tation,

             |A |G

You could dance   to a rock 'n' roll sta - tion.

       |D   G |

It was all right.

       |D   G |

It was all right.

                              ||

Oh, now here it comes right now.

Guitar Solo   D | C| | G| | D| | |

                D | C| | G| | D| | ||

Repeat 1st Verse

Chorus ||Em |G

De - spite all the amputa - tions,

       |A |G | ||

You could dance to a rock 'n' roll sta - tion.

Outro   D |C |D |C |

        D |C |D |C ||

Sic 'Em on a Chicken

Words and Music by
Zac Brown and John Driskell Hopkins

(Capo 3rd fret)

C   F   G   Am   E

Intro

| C | | |F | | |C | | |G | | |

| C | | |F | | |C | |G | |C | | ||

Chorus 1

C
Sic 'em on a chicken.
F
Sic 'em on a chicken.
C   G
Sic 'em on a chicken and watch them feathers fly.
C
Sic 'em on a chicken.
F
Sic 'em on a chicken.
C   G   C
Break out the butter and the flour; we're ready to fry.

Verse 2

C
My dog Pete's the smallest dog
  F
Of all the dogs in my yard. (That's right.)
  C
He's a mean sum-bitch, drinks Beam and water
  G
From a broken Mason jar.   And we

Repeat Chorus 1

Interlude 1   C | |F | |C | |G | |

                 C | |F | |C |G |C |

Verse 2

‖C | |
I heard this awful noise coming out of the woods.

F
      |
   (Coming out of the woods.)

      |C
I heard chicken screams.

 |C |G |
I knew it wasn't gonna be good.

Chorus 2

‖C |
I think we lost a chicken.

 |F |
I think we lost a chicken.

 |C | |G |
I think we lost a chicken 'cause I just heard her cry.

 |C |
I think we lost a chicken.

 |F |
I think we lost a chicken,

   |C |G |C | ‖
But you can get another one for a dollar seventy-nine.

Repeat Interlude 1

Verse 3

```
  ‖C                        |
Over a couple of years his spurs had grown,
  |F                        |
And he wasn't safe to keep    around the home.
   |C                     |
And he almost took an eye - ball
                    |G        |
From Lonny's son.
           |C                    |
And I was in the kitchen making fig preserves,
   |F                     |
And I heard that young'un got kicked in the face,
  |C                          |G
And I knew it was the day that that rooster's
                    |C          |
Gonna get what he de - serves.
```

Chorus 3

```
   ‖C              |           |
So I chased the chicken.
F                  |           |
I chased the chicken.
C                  |              |G      |        |
I chased the chicken and Pete hit him from the side.
C                  |        |
I chased the chicken.
F                  |        |
I chased the chicken.
C                      |G              |Am   |     |     |     ‖
Me and Pete suppered on a home-made chicken pot pie.
```

Interlude 2	Am											
	Am					|E	|Am		|Dm	|E Am	

Hey!

	Am					|E	|Am		|Dm	|E Am	

Hey!

	Am					|E	|Am		|Dm	|E Am	

Hey!

Am | | |E |Am | |Dm |E |

Am | | | |N.C. |

C | |F | |C | |G |

Chorus 4

‖C | |

Well, sic 'em on a chicken.

F | |

Sic 'em on a chicken.

C | |G | |

Sic 'em on a chicken and watch them feathers fly.

C | |

Sic 'em on a chicken.

F | |

Sic 'em on a chicken.

C |G |C | ‖

I can smell the kitchen and it's almost supper‑time.

Slow Dancing in a Burning Room

Words and Music by
John Mayer

(Capo 2nd fret)

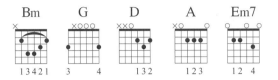

Bm   G   D   A   Em7

Intro

Bm |G   D |Bm |G   D |

Bm |G   D |Bm |G   D

Verse 1

‖Bm
It's not a silly little moment.
　　|G　　　　　　D
It's not the storm before the calm.
　　|Bm
This is the deep and dying breath of
　　　　　　　　|G　　　D
This love that we've been working on.
　　　|Bm
Can't seem to hold you like I want to
|G　　　　D
So I can feel you in my arms.
　|Bm
Nobody's gonna come and save you.
　　　　|G　　　D
We pulled too many false alarms.

Chorus

```
         ‖A
We're going  down,
         |Bm        G
And you can see it, too.
         |A
We're going  down,
         |Bm              Em7
And you know that we're doomed.
         |Bm                      |G     D     |
My dear,    we're slow dancing in a burning room.
Bm                 |G    D     |Bm            |G    D
```

Verse 2

```
         ‖Bm
I was the one you always dreamed of.
         |G              D
You were the one I tried to draw.
         |Bm
How dare you say it's nothing to me?
             |G           D
Baby, you're the only light I ever saw.
         |Bm
I'll make the most of all the sadness.
      |G                  D
You'll be a bitch because you can.
      |Bm
You try to hit me just to hurt me so you leave me feeling dirty,
      |G           D
'Cause you can't under - stand.
```

Repeat Chorus

Bridge

```
 ‖Em7        Bm                    |A        Em7
```
Go cry about it,   why don't you?

```
  |Em7        Bm                   |A        Em7
```
Go cry about it,   why don't you?

```
  |Em7        Bm                   |A        G
```
Go cry about it,   why don't you?

```
      |Bm                  |G        D          ‖
```
My dear,   we're slow dancing in a burning room.

Interlude

```
Bm              |G    D      |Bm              |G    D        |

Bm              |G    D      |Bm              |G    D
```


Outro

```
                          ‖Bm
```
Don't you think we oughta know by now?

```
                              |G                D
```
Don't you think we should have learned somehow?

```
                            |Bm
```
Don't you think we oughta know by now?

```
                              |G                D
```
Don't you think we should have learned somehow?

```
                            |Bm
```
Don't you think we oughta know by now?

```
                              |G                D            ‖
```
Don't you think we should have learned somehow?

The Sound of Silence

Words and Music by
Paul Simon

Am   G   C   F

Intro

Am |

Verse 1

Am   ‖G |
   Hello, darkness, my old friend;
G |Am |
   I've come to talk with you a - gain,
Am   C |F   C |
   Because a vision softly   creeping
C |F   C |
   Left it's seeds while I was   sleeping,
C |F | |C
   And the vision that was planted in my brain
       |C   Am |C |G |Am |
Still re - mains   within the sound of silence.

Verse 2

Am   ‖G |
   In restless dreams I walked a - lone,
G |Am |
   Narrow streets of cobble - stone.
Am   C |F   C |
   'Neath the halo of a   streetlamp,
C |F   C |
   I turned my collar to the cold and damp,
C |F | |C
   When my eyes were stabbed by the flash of a neon light
       |C   Am |C |G |Am |
That split the night   and touched the sound of silence.

Verse 3

Am   ‖G |
And in the naked light I saw

G |Am |
Ten thousand people, maybe more.

Am   C |F   C |
People talking without   speaking,

C |F   C |
People hearing without   listening,

C |F | |C
People writing songs that voices never share,

     |C   Am |C |G |Am |
And no one dare   disturb the sound of silence.

Verse 4

Am   ‖G |
"Fools!" said I, "You do not know

G |Am |
Silence like a cancer grows.

Am   C |F   C |
Hear my words that I might   teach you;

C |F   C |
Take my arms that I might   reach you."

C |F | |C | Am
But my words like silent raindrops fell,

   |C |G |Am |
And echoed in the wells of silence.

Verse 5

```
Am                           ‖G          |
    And the people bowed and prayed
G                        |Am         |
    To the neon god they made.
Am        C                  |F      C         |
    And the sign flashed out its   warning
C                        |F       C        |
    In the words that it was   forming,
C                        |F
    And the signs said, "The words of the prophets
    |F                        |C          |      Am
Are written on the subway walls   and tenement halls"
    |C              |G      |Am        |              ‖
And whispered in the sounds of silence.
```

Sunshine on My Shoulders

Words by John Denver
Music by John Denver, Mike Taylor and Dick Kniss

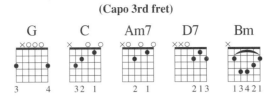

Chorus

G   C |G   C |G   C |G C |
Sunshine   on my shoulders   makes me happy,

G   C |G   C |Am7 |D7 |
Sunshine   in my eyes can make me cry.

G   C |G   C |G   C |G C |
Sunshine   on the water   looks so lovely,

G   C |G   C |G   C |G C ||
Sunshine   almost always   makes me high.

Verse 1

G   Am7 |Bm C |G   Am7 |Bm C
If I had a day   that I could give you,

|G   Am7 |Bm C |Am7   D7 |
I'd give to you   a day just like to-day.

G   Am7 |Bm C |G   Am7 |Bm C
If I had   a song   that I could sing for you,

|G   Am7 |Bm   C |G   Am7 |Bm C ||
I'd sing a song   to make you feel this way.

Repeat Chorus

Verse 2
```
G   Am7  |Bm C              |G      Am7  |Bm C
If I had a tale  that I could tell you,

     |G        Am7 |Bm  C           |Am7  |D7    |
I'd tell a tale       sure to make you smile.

G        Am7  |Bm  C             |G         Am7  |Bm  C
If I had     a wish  that I could wish for you,

    |G           Am7   |Bm       C    |G   Am7  |Bm C  ||
I'd make a wish       for sunshine all the while.
```

Repeat Chorus

Outro
```
G     C      |G        C          |G  Am7  |Bm C  |
Sunshine almost all the time  makes me high.              .

G     C      |G       C  |G Am7  |Bm C  G    ||
Sunshine almost always…
```

Sweet Child o' Mine

Words and Music by
W. Axl Rose, Slash, Izzy Stradlin', Duff McKagan and Steven Adler

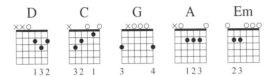

Verse 1

D
She's got a smile that it seems to me

    |C
Reminds   me of childhood   memories,

    |G   **|D**
Where ev - 'rything was as fresh   as the bright blue sky.

D
Now and then when I see her face,

    |C
She takes me away to that special place.

    |G   **|D**
And if I stared too long I'd probably break down and cry.

Chorus

A   **|C**   **|D**
Woh,   woh, woh, sweet child o' mine.

A   **|C**   **|D**
Woh, oh, oh, oh,   sweet love of mine.

Verse 2

  D |
She's got eyes of the bluest skies,

  |**C** |
As if they thought of rain.

  |**G** |
I'd hate to look in - to those eyes

   |**D** |
And see an ounce of pain.

   |**D** |
Her hair reminds me of a warm safe place

     |**C** |
Where as a child I'd hide

    |**G** |
And pray for the thunder   and the rain

     |**D** | ||
To qui - etly pass me by.

Repeat Chorus (2x)

Outro

Em   **|G** |
Where do we go?   Where do we go now?

A   **|C**   **D**   **G** |
Where do we go?

Em   **|G** |
Where do we go?   Where do we go now?

A   **|C**   **D**   **G** |
Where do we go?

Em   **|G** |
Where do we go?

A   **|C**   **D**   **G** |
Where do we go now?

Em   **|G** |
Where do we go?

A |
Where do we go now?

N.C.   **|Em**
No, no, no, no, no, no, no.

           |G   **|A** **|C**   **D** **|Em** ||
Sweet child,   sweet child   o' mine.

Sweet Jane

Words and Music by
Lou Reed

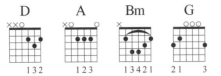

Intro

D   A |Bm   G   A |D   A |Bm   A   G   A |

D   A |Bm   G   A |D   A |Bm   A   G   A | ||

Verse 1

D   A |G   Bm   A |
Standing on the corner,

D   A |G   Bm   A |
Suit - case in my hand.

D   A |G   Bm   A |
Jack is in his corset; Jane is in her vest.

D   A |G   Bm   A |
And me, I'm in a rock 'n' roll band.

D   A |G   Bm   A |
Ride in a Stutz Bearcat, Jim.

D   A |G   Bm   A |
You know, those were different times.

D   A |G   Bm
Oh, all the poets, they studied rules of verse,

A |D   A |G   Bm   A ||
And those   ladies, they rolled their eyes.

Chorus

```
        D              |G          |
            Sweet Jane.
        D              |G          |
            Sweet Jane.
        D              |G          ||
            Sweet Jane.
```

Verse 2

```
        D                        A       |G      Bm      A      |
            I'll tell you somethin', that Jack, he is a banker,
        D         A  |G     Bm      A      |
            And Jane,     she is a clerk.
        D              A            |G        Bm      A      |
            And both of them save their    monies.
        D              A            |G              Bm      A      |
            And when, when they come home from work,
        D  A              |G      Bm      A      |
            Sittin' down by the fire,
        D          A    |G      Bm
            The radi - o does play
        A              |D
        A little classical music there, Jim:
            A          |G        Bm
        "The March of the Wooden Sol - diers."
        A              |D            A      |G  Bm  A          ||
        All you protest kids, you can hear Jack say,      "Get ready."
```

Repeat Chorus

79

	D	A		G	Bm	A		

Verse 3

```
        D   A        |G      Bm     A          |
          Some people,    they like to go out dancing,

        D           A      |G        Bm        A       |
          And other peo - ples, they have to work. Just watch me now.

        D           A          |G    Bm      A        |
          And there's even some evil moth - ers,

        D                   A       |G     Bm A       |
          Well, they're gonna tell you that every - thing is just   dirt.

        D              A    |G     Bm
          You know that wom - en never    really faint

        A      |D      A          |G    Bm A      |
        And that villains always blink their eyes

        D          A              |G      Bm       A        |
          And that, you know, children are the only ones who blush

        D          A    |G    Bm      A        ||
          And that life is just to die.
```

Bridge

```
        D              A     |G    Bm    A      |
          But anyone who ever had a heart,

        D          A             |G      Bm     A      |
        Oh, they wouldn't turn around and break it.

        D              A      |G     Bm     A      |
          And anyone who ever played a part,

        D            A           |G     Bm     A      ||
        Oh, they wouldn't turn around and hate it.
```

Repeat Chorus

The Unicorn

Words and Music by Shel Silverstein

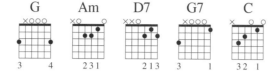

Verse 1

|G |Am
A long time ago, when the earth was green,

      |D7 |G
There was more kinds of animals than you've ever seen,

      |G   G7 |C
And they'd run around free while the earth was being born,

     |G |D7 G |
And the loveliest of all was the uni - corn.

Chorus 1

      ||G |Am |
There was green alligators and long - necked geese,

D7 |G |
Hump - back camels and chimpanzees,

G   G7 |C
Cats and rats and elephants, but sure as you're born,

  |G |D7 G |
The loveliest of all was the uni - corn.

Verse 2

    ‖**G** |**Am**
Lord seen some sinnin' and it caused him pain.

    |**D7** |**G**
He says, "Stand back, I'm gonna make it rain.

    |**G**   **G7** |**C**
So hey, Brother Noah, I'll tell you what to do,

      |**G**   **D7** |**G**
Go and build me a floating zoo."

Chorus 2

          ‖**G** |**Am**
"And you take two alligators and a couple of geese,

    |**D7** |**G**
Two hump - back camels and two chimpanzees,

    |**G**   **G7** |**C**
Two cats, two rats, two elephants, but sure as you're born,

    |**G** |**D7 G** |
Noah, don't you forget my uni - corns."

Verse 3

    ‖**G** |**Am**
Now, Noah was there and he answered the callin'

     |**D7** |**G**
And he finished up the ark as the rain started fallin',

     |**G**   **G7** |**C**
Then he marched in the animals two by two,

    |**G**   **D7** |**G**
And he sung as they went through:

Chorus 3

          ‖**G** |**Am**
"Hey, Lord, I've got you two alligators and a couple of geese,

    |**D7** |**G**
Two hump - back camels and two chimpanzees,

    |**G**   **G7** |**C**
Two cats, two rats, two elephants, but sure as you're born,

    |**G** |**D7 G** |
Lord, I just don't see your uni - corns."

Verse 4

    ‖G |Am

Well, Noah looked out through the drivin' rain,

      |D7 |G

But the unicorns was hidin', playin' silly games,

      |G   G7 |C |

They were kickin' and a-splashin' while the rain was pourin',

G |D7 G |

Oh, them foolish uni - corns.

Chorus 4

     ‖G |Am

I mean the two alligators and a couple of geese,

      |D7 |G |

The hump - back camels and the chimpanzees,

       |G   G7 |C

Noah cried, "Close the door 'cause the rain is pourin',

      |G |D7 G |

And we just can't wait for them uni - corns."

Verse 5

     ‖G |Am

And then the ark started movin' and it drifted with the tide,

      |D7 |G

And the unicorns looked up from the rock and cried,

      |G   G7 |C

And the water came up and sort of floated them away,

      |G |D7   G |

That's why you've never seen a uni - corn to this day.

Chorus 5

     ‖G |Am

You'll see a lot of alligators and a whole mess of geese,

      |D7 |G

You'll see hump - back camels and chimpanzees,

      |G   G7 |C

You'll see cats and rats and elephants, but sure as you're born,

      |G |D7 G | ‖

You're never gonna see no uni - corn.

Toes

Words and Music by
Zac Brown, Wyatt Durrette, John Driskell Hopkins and Shawn Mullins

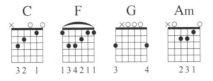

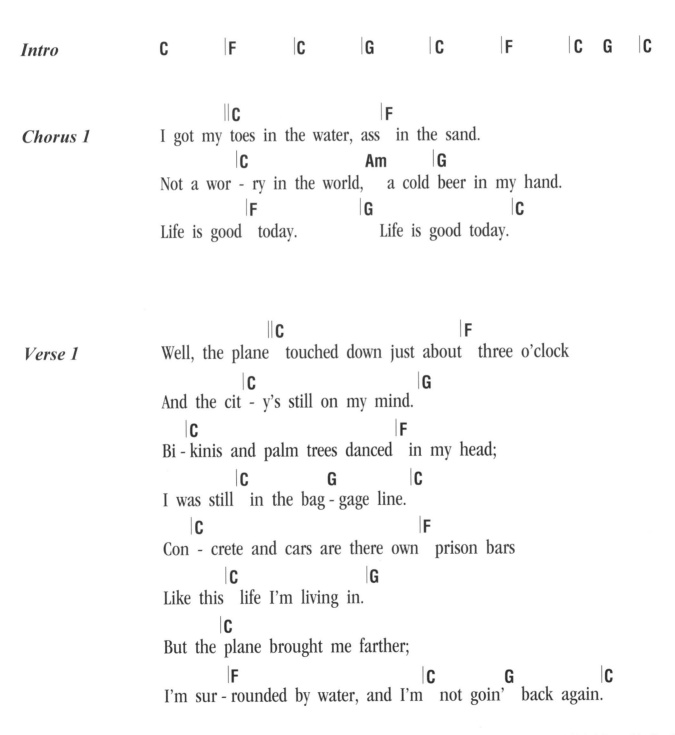

Intro C |F |C |G |C |F |C G |C

Chorus 1

‖C |F
I got my toes in the water, ass   in the sand.
          |C   Am |G
Not a wor - ry in the world,   a cold beer in my hand.
          |F |G |C
Life is good   today.   Life is good today.

Verse 1

          ‖C |F
Well, the plane   touched down just about   three o'clock
          |C |G
And the cit - y's still on my mind.
     |C |F
Bi - kinis and palm trees danced   in my head;
          |C   G |C
I was still   in the bag - gage line.
     |C |F
Con - crete and cars are there own   prison bars
          |C |G
Like this   life I'm living in.
          |C
But the plane brought me farther;
          |F |C   G |C
I'm sur - rounded by water, and I'm   not goin'   back again.

Chorus 2

‖**C** |**F**
I got my toes in the water, ass   in the sand.

          |**C**   **Am** |**G**
Not a wor - ry in the world,   a cold beer in my hand.

               |**F** |**G** |**C** |
Life is good   today.   Life is good today.

Bridge 1

C Tacet |**F** |
   Adios and vaya con Dios.

F |**C** |
   Yeah, I'm leaving GA.

                         |**G** |
And if it weren't   for tequila and pretty señoritas,

   |**G** |**C** |
I'd,   I'd have no reason to stay.

C Tacet |**F** |
   Adios and vaya con Dios,

F |**C** |
   Yeah, I'm leaving GA.

          |**G** | |
Gonna lay in the hot sun and roll a big fat one and,

G Tacet |**C** |**F** |
   And grab my guitar and play.

C |**G** |**C** |**F** |**C** **G** |**C**

Verse 2

                ‖**C** |**F**
Well, four days flew by like a drunk Friday night

          |**C** |**G**
As the sum - mer drew to an end.

    |**C** |**F**
They can't believe that I just couldn't leave,

      |**C**   **G** |**C**
And I bid adieu to my friends.

       |**C** |**F**
'Cause my bartender, she's from the islands;

    |**C** |**G**
Her body's been kissed by the sun.

    |**C** |**F**
And coconut replaces the smell of the bar,

       |**C**   **G** |**C**
And I don't know if its her or the rum.

Repeat Chorus 2

Bridge 2

C Tacet   ‖**F** |
  Adios and vaya con Dios.

F |**C** |
  A long way from GA.

        |**G** | |
Yes, and all the muchachas, they call me "Big Poppa"

G |**C** |
  When I throw pesos their way.

C Tacet |**F** |
  Adios and vaya con Dios.

F |**C** |
  A long way from GA.

       |**G** | |
Someone do me a favor and pour me some Jaeger and

G Tacet |**C** |**F** |
  I'll grab my guitar and play.

C |**G** |**C** |**F** |**C** **G** |**C**   ‖

Bridge 3

C Tacet   **‖F** |

   Adios and vaya con Dios,

F   **|C** |

   Going home now to stay.

       |G | |

The seño - ritas don't *quiero* when there's no *dinero*, yeah,

G   **|C** |

   And I got no money to stay.

C Tacet   **|F** |

   Adios and vaya con Dios,

F   **|C** | ‖

   Going home now to stay.

Chorus 3

G |

  Just gonna drive up by the lake,

     |C   **|F**

And put my ass in a lawn chair, toes in the clay.

    |C   **Am** **|G**

Not a wor - ry in the world,   a PB - R on the way.

     |F   **|G**   **|C**   **|F** **G** **C**   ‖

Life is good today.   Life is good today.

Tonight, Not Again

Words and Music by
Jason Mraz and Jenny Keane

(Capo 3rd fret)

Em(add2) Fsus2 Gsus2 F C

1 4   1 3 4   2 1 3   1 3 4 2 1 1   3 2 1

Intro   Em(add2)|Fsus2 |Em(add2)|Fsus2 |Em(add2)|Fsus2 |Em(add2)|Fsus2

Verse 1

‖Em(add2) |Fsus2 |
The night,   she brushed her hand upon my   flushed cheek;

Em(add2) |Fsus2 |
          Smelled of childhood, remnants of a dust - y weeping willow.

Em(add2) |Fsus2
          Clouds soothe, they're shredded by the calico;

|Em(add2) |Fsus2 |
Were oh so vast and quick as I was on   my own now.

Em(add2) |Fsus2 |Em(add2) |Fsus2   ‖

Verse 2

Em(add2) |Fsus2 |
          And this time, like every other time,   I believe that I never find

Em(add2) |Fsus2 |
          Another sweet little girl with sequined sea   foam eyes,

Em(add2) |Fsus2 |Em(add2)
Ocean-lapping voice, smile coy as the brightest quiet span of   sky.

                          |Fsus2
And I'm all alone again   tonight.

                  |Em(add2) |Fsus2
Not again, not again, not again.

                  |Em(add2) |Fsus2
Not again, not again, not   again. Mm.

Chorus 1

```
     ‖Gsus2        |                              |F
Mm,            oo.              And don't it feel al - right?
                        |C
And don't it feel so   nice?
     |Gsus2              |F            |C                  |Em(add2)
Love  -  ly,   love  -  ly,   love  -  ly. Say, say it again.
     |Fsus2                  |Em(add2)  |Fsus2
Ah,        lovely. Say it again.          Ah.
```

Verse 3

```
     ‖Em(add2)         |Fsus2
Well, I'm          unable to inhale all the riches
     |Em(add2)                           |Fsus2
As I'm          awkward as a wound on my bones.
          |Em(add2)                      |Fsus2
Still, I've got      cobblestone joints and plate glass points,
     |Em(add2)                   |Fsus2
As I'm all by myself tonight. Not a - gain, not again.
```

Chorus 2

```
     ‖Gsus2        |                              |F
Oo,            oo.              And don't it feel al - right?
                        |C
And don't it feel so   nice?
     |Gsus2              |F            |C
Love  -  ly,   love  -  ly,   love  -  ly.
     |Gsus2              |
Say-ay  -   ay  -  ay - ay.
```

Bridge

                      ‖**F** |**C**
And if you should   nervously break down when its time for the shakedown,

          |**Gsus2**
Would you   take it?

               |**F** |**C**
It's when you cry just a little but you laugh in the middle

         |**Gsus2**
That you've   made it.

                 |**F** |**C**
And don't it feel al - right? And don't it feel so nice?

    |**Gsus2** | |**F** |**C** |
Love,   love, love, love. *Scat sing...*

Gsus2 | |**F** |**C**

Interlude

                      ‖**Em(add2)** |**Fsus2** |**Em(add2)**
Say it, say it, say it again.   Love,   love.

     |**Fsus2** |**Em(add2)** |**Fsus2** |**Em(add2)** |**Fsus2**
Love.   Love,   so lovely,   lovely to do it again.

     |**Em(add2)** |**Fsus2** |**Em(add2)** |**Fsus2**
It's so love - ly to do it again.

     |**Em(add2)** |**Fsus2**
Again,   oh, loving again.

          |**Em(add2)** |**Fsus2** |**Gsus2** | |
It's coming again.   It's coming again.

F |**C** |**Gsus2** | |**F** |**C** |**Gsus2** |**F** |**C**
Scat sing...

Outro

```
                                    ‖Em(add2)        |Fsus2
Say it, say it, say it again.              Oh,
     |Em(add2)          |Fsus2          |Em(add2)
So            beautiful.        Tonight,
                      |Fsus2        |Em(add2)        |Fsus2        |
It's coming again.        Love,              lovely.
Em(add2)                   |Fsus2        |Em(add2)  |Fsus2        |
Love,  love. Scat sing...
Em(add2)        |Fsus2        |Em(add2)        |Fsus2        ‖
                                    Lovely.
```

Turn! Turn! Turn!
(To Everything There Is a Season)

Words from the Book of Ecclesiastes
Adaptation and Music by Pete Seeger

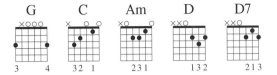

Chorus

|G   C |G   Am |
To every - thing, turn, turn, turn,

|G   C |G   Am |
There is a season, turn, turn, turn,

|D |D7
And a time to every purpose

|G |
Under heaven.

Verse 1

||D7 |G
A time to be born, a time to die,

|D7 |G
A time to plant, a time to reap,

|D7 |G
A time to kill, a time to heal,

|C |D7 |G |
A time to laugh, a time to weep.

Repeat Chorus

Verse 2

```
              ‖D7                        |G
A time to build up, a time to break down,

              |D7              |G         |
A time to dance, a time to mourn,

D7                      |G
A time to cast away stones,

              |C       |D7        |G          |
A time to gather stones to - gether.
```

Repeat Chorus

Verse 3

```
              |D7              |G
A time of war, a time of peace,

              |D7              |G
A time of love, a time of hate,

D7                      |G
A time you may em - brace,

  |C              |D7              |G          |
A time to re - frain from em - bracing.
```

Repeat Chorus

Verse 4

```
              ‖D7              |G
A time to gain, a time to lose,

              |D7              |G
A time to rend, a time to sew,

              |D7              |G
A time of love, a time of hate,

          |C       |D7              |G      |       ‖
A time for peace, I swear it's not too late.
```

Vultures

Words and Music by
John Mayer, Pino Paladino and Steven Jordan

(Capo 2nd fret)

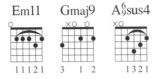

Intro   **Em11** | | | | | | | ‖

Verse 1

Em11 | |
Some of us, we're hardly ever here.

Em11 | |
The rest of us, we're born to disappear.

Em11 | |
How do I stop myself from being just a number?

Em11 | ‖
How will I hold my head to keep from going under?

Chorus 1

Gmaj9 |
Down to the wire   I wanted water

|**A⁶₉sus4** |
But I'll walk through the fire.   If this is what it takes

|**Gmaj9** | |**A⁶₉sus4**
To take me even higher,   then I'll come through like I do

|**A⁶₉sus4**
When the world keeps testing me, testing me,

|**Em11** | | | ‖
Testing   me.

Verse 2

Em11 | |

How did they find me here? What do they want from me?

Em11 | |

All of these vultures hiding right outside my door,

Em11 | |

I hear them whispering. They're trying to ride it out.

Em11 | ||

They've never gone this long with - out a kill before.

Repeat Chorus 1

Interlude 1 Em11 | | | | | | | |

         Gmaj9 | |Em11 | |Gmaj9 | |Em11 | ||

Verse 3

Em11 | |

Wheels up, I got to leave this evening.

Em11 | |

I can't seem to shake these vultures off of my trail.

Em11 | |

Power is made by power being taken.

Em11 | ||

So I keep on running to pro - tect my situation.

Chorus 2

Gmaj9 |

Down to the wire I wanted water

    |A$_9^6$sus4 |

But I'll walk through the fire. If this is what it takes

   |Gmaj9 | |A$_9^6$sus4

To take me even higher, then I'll come through like I do

      |A$_9^6$sus4 ||

When the world keeps testing me, testing me.

Interlude 2

Gmaj9		A⁶₉sus4		
Whoo,		whoo.		

Gmaj9		A⁶₉sus4		‖
Whoo,		whoo.		

Outro

Em11

What you gonna do about it? What you gonna do about it?

Em11

What you gonna do about it?

|Em11

Don't   give up, give up.

|Em11

Don't   give up, give up, give up.

|Em11

Don't   give up, give up.

|Em11

Don't   give up, give up, give up.

Waiting on the World to Change

Words and Music by
John Mayer

D   Bm   G   A   Em7

Intro

D   Bm |G   D |A   Bm |G   D ||

Verse 1

      D   Bm |G   D
Me and all my friends, we're all   misunder - stood.
   |A   Bm |G   D
They say we stand for nothing and there's no way we ever could.
       |D   Bm
Now we see   everything that's going wrong
 |G   D
With the world and those who lead it.
   |A   Bm |G   D
We just feel like we don't   have the means to rise above and beat it.

Chorus 1

    ||D   Bm |G   D
So we keep waiting (waiting), waiting on the world to change.
  |A   Bm |G   D
We keep on waiting (waiting), waiting on the world to change.
 |D   Em7 |Bm   Em7
It's hard to beat the system when we're standing at a distance.
  |A   Bm |G   D
So we keep waiting (waiting), waiting on the world to change.

97

Verse 2

```
      ‖D                  Bm                    |G              D
Now, if we had the power to bring our neigh - bors home from war,
               |A          Bm              |G              D
They would have never missed a Christmas; no more ribbons on their door.
               |D               Bm          |G              D
And when you trust your tele - vision, what you get is what you got.
               |A             Bm                |G              D
'Cause when they own the infor - mation, oh, they can bend it all they want.
```

Chorus 2

```
                  ‖D  Bm                    |G              D
That's why we're wait - ing (waiting), waiting on the world to change.
          |A     Bm                |G              D
We keep on waiting (waiting), waiting on the world to change.
 |D                Em7          |Bm              Em7
It's not that we don't care; we just know    that the fight ain't    fair.
          |A     Bm                |G              D
So we keep on waiting (waiting), waiting on the world to change.
```

Chorus 3

```
                  ‖D     Bm                    |G              D
And we're still waiting (waiting), waiting on the world to change.
          |A     Bm                |G              D
We keep on waiting (waiting), waiting on the world to change.
 |D                Em7          |Bm              Em7
One day our gener - ation is gonna rule the popu - lation.
          |A     Bm                |G              D
So we keep on waiting (waiting), waiting on the world to change.
```

Outro

|| **A**   **Bm** | **G**   **D**

I know we keep on waiting (waiting), waiting on the world to change.

| **A**   **Bm** | **G**   **D**

We keep on waiting (waiting), we're waiting on the world to change.

| **G**   **D**

Waiting on the world to change.

| **G**   **D**

Waiting on the world to change.

| **G**   **D** ||

Waiting on the world to change.

Walk on the Wild Side

Words and Music by
Lou Reed

Tune down one whole step:
(low to high) D-G-C-F-A-D

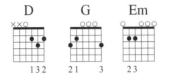

Intro   D |G |D |G |D |G |D |G   ‖

Verse 1

D |G |
Holly came from Miami, F - L - A,

D |G |
Hitchhiked her way across the U.S. - A.

D   Em |
Plucked her eyebrows on   the way,

G   Em
Shaved her legs and then he was a she.

        |D |G
She says, "Hey, babe, take a walk on the wild   side."

        |D |G |
Said, "Hey, honey, take a walk on the wild   side."

D |G |D |G   ‖

Verse 2

D |G |

Candy came from out on the island.

D |G |

In the backroom, she was everybody's darling.

D   Em |

But she never lost   her head,

G   Em

Even when she was givin' head.

         |D |G

She says, "Hey, babe, take a walk on the wild   side."

         |D |G

Said, "Hey, babe, take a walk on the wild   side."

                    ||

And the colored girls go:

Chorus

D |

Do, do-do, do-do, do-do-do.

G |

Do, do-do, do-do, do-do-do.

D |

Do, do-do, do-do, do-do-do.

G |

Do, do-do, do-do, do-do-do.

D |

(Do, do-do, do-do, do-do-do.)

G |

(Do, do-do, do-do, do-do-do.)

D |

(Do, do-do, do-do, do-do-do.)

G |

(Do, do-do, do-do, do-do-do.)

D |G |D |G ||

(Do.)

Verse 3

D |G |
Little Joe never once gave it away.

D |G
Everybody had to pay and pay.

 |D   Em |
A hustle here and a hustle there.

G   Em
New York City is the   place where

            |D |G
They said, "Hey, babe, take a walk on the wild   side."

          |D |G |
I said, "Hey, Joe, take a walk on the wild   side."

D |G |D |G ||

Verse 4

D |G |
Sugar Plum Fairy came and hit the streets,

D |G |
Lookin' for soul food and a place to eat.

D   Em
Went to the Apollo;

 |G   Em
You should have seen him go - go-go.

         |D |G
They said, "Hey, Sugar, take a walk on the wild   side."

        |D |G
I said, "Hey, babe, take a walk on the wild   side."

         |D |G   D |G ||
All right,   huh.

Verse 5

```
      D                        |G              |
      Jackie is just speeding away.
      D                               |G         |
      Thought she was James Dean for a day.
      D                    Em         |
      Then I guess she had    to crash;
      G               Em
      Valium would have helped that bash.
               |D                          |G
      She said, "Hey, babe, take a walk on the wild   side."
               |D                          |G
      I said, "Hey, honey, take a walk on the wild   side."
                                  ||
      And the colored girls say:
```

Repeat Chorus

Walk Right In

Words and Music by Gus Cannon and H. Woods

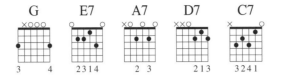

Verse 1

G | **E7** |
Walk right in, set right down,

A7 **D7** |**G** |
Daddy, let your mind roll on.

G | **E7** |
Walk right in, set right down,

A7 |**D7** |
Daddy, let your mind roll on.

G | |
Everybody's talkin' 'bout a new way of walkin'.

C7 | **D7** |
Do you want to lose your mind?

G | **E7** |
Walk right in, set right down,

A7 **D7** |**G** ||
Daddy, let your mind roll on.

Verse 2

G | **E7** |
Walk right in, set right down,

A7 **D7** |**G** |
Baby, let your hair hang down.

G | **E7** |
Walk right in, set right down,

A7 |**D7** |
Baby, let your hair hang down.

G | |
Everybody's talkin' 'bout a new way of walkin'.

C7 | **D7** |
Do you want to lose your mind?

G | **E7** |
Walk right in, set right down,

A7 **D7** |**G** **E7** |
Baby, let your hair hang down.

A7 **D7** |**G** ‖
Baby, let your hair hang down.

We Shall Overcome

Words based on 1901 hymn by C. Albert Findley entitled "I'll Overcome Some Day"
Music based on 1794 hymn entitled "O Sanctissima"

```
  C        F        Am       D        G
```

Verse 1

```
C        F      |C    |        F    |C    |
We shall over - come, we shall over - come,

C        F      |Am  D |G        D  |G
We shall over - come some day,

   |C    F    |C    |F  G  |Am           |
Oh, deep in my heart, I do be - lieve,

C        F    |C    G |C   F  |C    ||
We shall over - come some day.
```

Verse 2

```
C        F      |C    |        F    |C    |
We'll walk hand in hand, we'll walk hand in hand,

C        F      |Am  D |G        D  |G
We'll walk hand in hand some day,

   |C    F    |C    |F  G  |Am           |
Oh, deep in my heart, I do be - lieve,

C        F    |C    G |C   F  |C    ||
We shall over - come some day.
```

Verse 3

```
C       F    |C   |      F    |C        |
```
We are not a - fraid, we are not a - fraid,

```
C       F    |Am  D |G    D    |G
```
We are not a - fraid to - day,

```
    |C   F    |C   |F G  |Am       |
```
Oh, deep in my heart, I do be - lieve,

```
C       F    |C   G |C   F    |C      ||
```
We shall over - come some day.

Verse 4

```
C       F    |C   |      F    |C        |
```
We shall stand to - gether, we shall stand to - gether,

```
C       F    |Am  D |G    D    |G
```
We shall stand to - geth - er now,

```
    |C   F    |C   |F G  |Am       |
```
Oh, deep in my heart, I do be - lieve,

```
C       F    |C   G |C   F    |C      ||
```
We shall over - come some day.

More Great Piano/Vocal Books

FROM CHERRY LANE

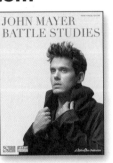

For a complete listing of Cherry Lane titles available, including contents listings, please visit our web site at

www.cherrylane.com

See your local music dealer or contact:

cherry lane
music company

EXCLUSIVELY DISTRIBUTED BY
HAL•LEONARD® CORPORATION

7777 W. BLUEMOUND RD. P.O. BOX 13819 MILWAUKEE, WI 53213

Prices, contents and availability subject to change without notice.

1112